INTRODUCTION

Of all of the cats that you might select from, the Siamese is what I would term the quintessential cat: this elegant, lithe feline has been the subject of many myths and legends throughout the ages, and it remains among the most popular breeds of cat.

independent nature is the source of mixed feelings among humans. The confirmed dog lover sees the cat as a rather disloyal creature that is essentially untrainable, therefore of little use. There are also those who are fearful of cats. The feline stare suggests it has

Like the statues of the cats of ancient Egypt, the Siamese is regal and worthy of all of the finer things in life.

The cat is an independent creature that has fascinated humans for a few thousand years. It makes few demands upon its owner, only that it is given a warm place to live, sound nutrition, and a measure of general care and kindness. It will repay you with a great deal of affection, and much more than this, no cat owner expects.

It cannot be stated that the cat will be suited to everyone. Its very

some uncanny mystical powers that can in some way look right into a person's inner self — it makes some people nervous in the presence of these animals. This aspect of the cat has meant that from its earliest association with humans, it has been surrounded by myths and legends.

To the cat lover, felines are the epitome of the ideal pet. In it they see a creature of elegant proportions that is quiet, undemanding, highly intelligent, and loyal. They admire the high level of independence of this group of predators, regarding it as a sure sign of its special status as a pet that is not "owned" in quite the same way that all others are. There is then a third group of people who neither worship nor dislike cats. They see them for what they are — small predatory animals that can survive quite well without humans, but can be very useful to us in helping to control rodent populations. The farmer is probably the best example of this group, for I doubt you will ever come across a ranch or any other farm based business that does not maintain at least one or two resident cats. Indeed, it was probably this latter group of people who first brought about the domestication of cats in Egypt about 1,500 B.C.

If you are the sort of person who has a neutral view of felines, be assured this will quickly become one of ardent cat lover. Even those who had professed no great affinity for these pets have been converted once they had actually taken one into their home.

This book is about just one breed — the Siamese. In many ways, these oriental cats represent the extremes of a domestic cat, with the Persian possibly being at the other extreme. While the latter is a cobby, longcoated, quiet and relatively docile feline, the Siamese is its opposite. It is a lithe, shortcoated, vocal, and extremely active cat. It makes its presence obvious by its outgoing nature. All other breeds can be said to be somewhere between the extremes seen in these cats. More than any others, the Persian and the Siamese have shaped the development of the modern day domestic cat fancy.

Allowing your Siamese to roam freely outdoors increases the chances of its getting injured or contracting a disease.

FROM WILD TO DOMESTIC

No one knows for sure when the cat was first domesticated because the process in any species has never been documented. All that can be done is to study our own history and try to draw logical conclusions on how our association with various creatures probably arose. The first thing that can be established is that humans started to domesticate an animal only when

From its humble beginnings as a rodent catcher, the Siamese cat went on to become adored by many people and even worshipped by some cultures.

it offered a practical advantage. Thus the first domesticated species was probably the dog, which was a hunter whose social organization was very similar to that of early nomads. It was easily integrated into human settlements because its way of life was comparable to ours — we merely became its new "pack."

Following the dog came sheep, chickens and fowl, cattle, camels, and horses. The cat was a relatively late arrival on the domestic scene because it lived a rather solitary life, was extremely ferocious, and had little to gain from associating itself with humans. Further, cats are very territorial and had no inclination to follow nomadic people. The situation started to change once humans settled and created fixed encampments. Two major happenings then resulted. First, where there are many people there will always be garbage, and where there is garbage there will be rodents — mice and rats. Second, fixed settlements resulted in agriculture, which is not a feature of a nomadic way of life and resulted in an increase in the population of rodents. It is these two facts that probably brought the cat onto the scene. Wild cats found that by staying near to human settlements, they were assured of a very steady supply of food in the form of rodents as well as in any other bits of meat that came their way for one reason or another.

In turn, humans would quickly see the advantages of encouraging cats to stay in the area in order to help reduce the numbers of rodents, whose populations grew in direct proportion to the increased grain harvests and garbage created by the humans. Sooner or later, some kittens would be captured. Of these, any which had a less wild character than the average, would no doubt have stayed within the encampment to breed with others of a similar nature. The genetic process of domestication was thus underway.

THE CAT CULTURE

The Egyptians, like all early civilizations, had many deities. Each of these was worshipped in many forms; each form being more popular in one area than in another. The lion was the first of the cat gods and was worshipped as Tefnut in Heliopolis and as Sekhmet in Memphis. In Bubastis, a city in Lower Egypt, the lioness goddess was Bast or Bastet. With the passage of time, the lioness was replaced by the domestic cat to represent Bast, though in some cities the lioness remained the only form of this goddess.

Bast had her ups and downs because at one point the pharaoh Amenhotop IV banned all old gods, but these were reinstated by Tutankhamen, his successor. Thereafter, there was a steady rise in the worship of many animal gods, and a steady decline in the power of the pharaohs as the reincarnation of god on earth. With the passage of time, Bast emerged as the most important deity, possibly reaching her peak

The Siamese, more than any other breed, has been instrumental in the creation of new cat breeds. Siamese-like qualities are readily apparent in this Colorpoint Shorthair.

during the years that followed the Libyan rulers of Egypt making Bubastis the capital of the Lower Kingdom about 1,000 B.C.

Cats were either mummified or cremated following their death, though some were also ritually killed in temples. The followers of Bast took stringent measures against those who might harm the cat. Many people were tortured or killed for such crimes. The annual festival of Bast at the capital is thought to have been one of the largest of all festivals. It attracted devotees from all over Egypt. Estimates are that over 600,000 gathered, and the ceremonies were accompanied with much merriment, orgies, and worship. Mummified temple cats could be purchased, and these were highly valued by followers of the cult. The cult remained a strong one in Egypt until the last Cleopatra's (VII) rule was replaced by the Roman Emperors in 30 B.C. Thereafter, though it survived well for some centuries, it started to lose momentum, no doubt due to the fact that the Romans elevated their own gods to the highest positions. It was eventually banned when Theodosius declared Rome and her provinces Christian. Notwithstanding this, even today, there are those who still secretly believe in the old gods of Egypt.

THE SPREAD OF THE CAT

From Egypt, the cat steadily spread both east and west via the traders of Egypt and Phoenicia. It probably arrived in Britain during the early years of the first century A.D. During the next few hundred years, the lot of the cat remained quite good, but it took a sinister turn with changes in social and religious beliefs that came about during the Middle Ages in Europe. From about 1,000 A.D., the cat became associated with witchcraft and for the next 800 years became subjected to horrific cruelty on which we will not dwell. Surprisingly, even during this very bad period in the history of the cat, some managed to lead quite good lives — much depending on how important the owner was!

From Britain and other sea faring nations, such as France, Spain, and Holland, the cat was

The Siamese, like other breeds of cat, will devote a good deal of time to a favorite cat activity—cat napping!

Cats are very territorial animals. This Siamese is perched on its scratching post, giving its claws a good workout.

Kittens love to nap together and will often display affection for one another with a nudge.

Above: The Siamese is an expressive feline. Its big, blue eyes and sharp facial features display intelligence and wisdom.

Below: Provide your Siamese kitten with all the proper care and all the creature comforts it deserves.

transported to the New World, to Australia, and to many island states. Everywhere it was taken it adapted and prospered — even in the sub arctic and antarctic regions of our planet. With the staging of the world's first cat show in England during 1871, the cat was to commence on the path that was to regain its status as a highly prized domestic resident. At that very first cat show was a Siamese.

The cat has thus had a checkered history in which it has been worshipped and persecuted. To this day, the quality of its life will very much depend on which country it happens to be born and into what sort of a home it will end up. In this book, you will find all of the information that you will need in order to ensure that its life in your home will be one of contentment and mutual enjoyment for both the cat and your family.

BREED HISTORY AND CHARACTER

The history of the Siamese cat can be divided into two quite distinct eras. The first we know virtually nothing about, as it relates to the origins of the breed type. The second era details the development of the breed since it first made its appearance in Europe.

No one knows for sure when the Siamese type, which in cats is termed "foreign", came into being. Various authorities over the years have theorized that these foreign breeds arose as a result of crossings between the original Egyptian cats and wild cats native to Eastern countries. Others believe that they are the result of a mutation through which all present day breeds have arisen and the subsequent crossings between these and other existing breeds of any given period of time.

Exactly when such mutations happened can only be guessed at because there are no written records. We can gain some insight from evidence presented in the form of art. For example, there exists in Thailand, formerly Siam, a series of illustrated poems that depict the cat breeds known to exist at the time the poems were written. Some 17 breeds are covered, including the Siamese, the Korat, and the Copper or Burmese. It is difficult to be precise as to which breeds are actually being depicted because the illustrations can hardly be regarded as anything but crude.

The unique "foreign" body shape of the Siamese was embraced by Europeans in the 18th century.

The date of these poem scripts is also far from certain. What we do know is that they could have been written anytime between 1350 and 1767, a rather wide span of time. Even so, this does tell us that the Siamese and the foreign breeds in general were in existence for some centuries before they were recognized in Europe. That they had not been brought to Europe is not surprising, given the fact that throughout this period in the

West the cat was the subject of religious persecution that did not abate until the 18th century.

It is thought that the original Egyptian domestic cats arrived in Thailand, Burma, and China as a result of the silk trade routes that date back into antiquity. Also, there were sea routes from Arabia to India, and thence across the Bay of Bengal to Burma and Thailand. All present day theories on the domestication of the cat do assume this took place in Egypt, but we should never overlook the possibility that there may well have been two or more centers of domestication. It then became a case that the one in Egypt was given greater impetus and importance due to the fact that the Egyptians made the cat a deity in the form of the cat goddess Bast. In other areas, the cat did not reach this status, so it was not considered important to document its existence.

THE MODERN ERA

Beginning in the 19th century, there were dramatic social changes in Europe. One result of these was that there developed a great interest in the study of natural history. Societies devoted to the preservation of old domestic species came into being. Others were devoted to the creation of new interest areas. The cat became subject to both of these. In 1871, Harrison Weir, regarded as the Father of the Cat Fancy, organized a show of domestic and foreign cats, which took place in

Let's not fight over nomenclature! In some registries, Siamese are registerable with lynx point markings.

If you own a fish tank, watch your Siamese cat very carefully. Cats are fascinated by fish and could fall in the tank or knock it over.

the Crystal Palace (now no more) on July 13th. The show proved a tremendous success, a result of which the cat fancy came into being.

There were a total of 25 classes, and among the breeds exhibited were a pair of Siamese. The *Graphic*, reporting on the show, stated that the Siamese cats were "soft fawn colored creatures with jet black legs, an unnatural nightmare kind of cat." Another paper described them as "singular and elegant in their smooth skins." They stated that the cat had "ears tipped with black and blue eyes with red pupils." Yet

another observer regarded them as being like black-faced pugs. An illustration of them along with breeds such as the Persian and others appeared in the *Graphics* July 22nd issue.

Interest in the Siamese Temple Cats, as they were sometimes referred to, grew rapidly in Britain but was much slower in mainland Europe. The breed reached the USA from Britain, and the first cat registered in the States was in 1879. It was, however, to be a few years later before the cat really took off in the USA.

In 1884, a pair of cats arrived in England that had been given to the British Consul General, Owen Gould, by the King of Siam. These and the cats shown three years earlier at Crystal Palace were not like the Siamese cats of today. They were stockier in build and remain so to this day in their homeland. It would seem that in Siam there existed two races of Siamese cats — those of the streets and those owned by the nobility (the Royal Siamese).

Legend has it that the dark areas on the neck of the Siamese are the shadow, left in perpetuity, from a time in the past when a god picked up one of these cats. It is also said that when a member of the royal family died, a Siamese cat (though not necessarily of the breed we are discussing) was entombed alive with its royal master. Some holes were made in the lid of the tomb, and when the cat eventually emerged from one, it was considered that the spirit of the deceased had passed into the cat. Similar legends of the cat being a home for the souls of people are very common in numerous Far Eastern countries.

Another legend surrounding the Siamese and other cats of that country is that the tail kink, which was and remains common in the tail of many of these cats, was placed there in order that when the princesses of the monarch were bathing they would have somewhere on which to hang their rings. In reality, the kink is the result of a genetic flaw that was obviously inherent in the original gene pool of the cats of foreign build. It was originally a desired feature of the Siamese

when it arrived in Europe but was later to be classed as a fault, as it is today in exhibition stock.

By the turn of the century, the Siamese was attracting a considerable number of devotees, so it was logical that specialty clubs would be formed. The first of these was in England in 1901, and an official standard of excellence followed a year later. In the USA, the Siamese Club was created in 1909. The first All Siamese show in England took place in 1924. Its counterpart in the USA happened in 1928, and in that same year, the financial adviser to the King of Siam attended the fifth English specialty Siamese show and awarded prizes from the monarch of that country.

Although the Siamese was very popular in the USA as this century began to unfurl, the same was not so in Canada, where the first show in 1906 featured none of the breed. It was to be a few years later before the breed became very popular. The breed was seen at early Australian shows (which were not just devoted to cats) where a pair were exhibited as early as 1901.

In France, the first shows were in the 1890s. The Siamese rapidly gained followers to the degree that in the all-breed shows of the first years of this century, the Siamese was already suggesting that it would become an extremely popular breed—a vision that became reality. Indeed, only the Persian has consistently bettered its numbers either as a pet or a show specimen over the years.

The Siamese has been welcomed in the homes of people around the globe. In the US and Canada, the Siamese counts among the most popular cats.

Today the breed is at a sort of crossroads in its development because there is much controversy over the breeding policies adopted in Western nations over the years. There is no doubt that the difference between a winning show specimen and some typical pets is very considerable. The exhibitor favors an extremely lithe cat, whereas the average pet owner will probably prefer a cat with more substance to its body. There is no doubt that in concentrating effort towards an ever-slimmer cat with a more pronounced wedge to the face has resulted in problems within the breed. This will have to be addressed by future breeders and judges, or the Siamese will be destined for a rapid decline. It is thus both an interesting and challenging time for those entering the breed.

Seal Point Siamese exhibiting the posture typical of a cat stalking prey.

THE SIAMESE CHARACTER

The Siamese is the ultimate feline extrovert. Its characteristics are so different from the average cat's that it is often described as being almost dog like. This is a very affectionate breed that displays its moods more obviously than most, which in no way detracts from other breeds. It has a wide range of sounds and is extremely intelligent. This fact no doubt accounts for its ability to be mischievous around the home. Cats are not animals that take kindly to lead training — they are not dogs after all — but the Siamese probably accepts lead training better than most felines.

The ideal Siamese owner must definitely be the sort of person who wants a very close association with their cat. The breed is very vocal and will respond well to those who do not mind its constant talking. It is a very elegant, athletic cat, however, it is not quite as bad as its reputation sometimes suggests for creating havoc in the home! It will only charge over your furniture and up the curtains if it is allowed to "take over" the home or if you leave it for long periods with nothing to do but to find things to do itself. Any cat can get bored if it is denied companionship for long hours. Whereas many will content themselves with simply sleeping the time away, a Siamese will devise ways of amusing itself, especially when it is young.

As stated earlier, the Siamese is the opposite of the Persian in just about all of its features. If you want a quiet, sedate feline, then obtain a Persian; if you want a cat that lets you know it's around, the Siamese is the one for you.

Cats and dogs can get along very well if they are brought up together from an early age.

SELECTING A SIAMESE CAT

THE QUALITY OF YOUR PET

Siamese come in a range of qualities from the inferior, through the typical examples of the breed, to those which are show winners, or at least potentially so. You may wish to own a high-quality Siamese even though you have no intention to show it. Quality means it will have good bone conformation, the correct stature, and its color or patterns will be of a high standard. Such a cat will be a costly purchase. A typical Siamese will be just that. It will display no glaring faults and its color will be sound. It may display some minor failings in type or color that would preclude it from ever being of show quality.

An inferior Siamese will be one which has obvious faults, either its conformation, its coat quality, poor color or in other ways inferior. Such cats are often described as being pet quality. As long as you appreciate that this term means inferior, its use is fine. However, there are two kinds of inferior Siamese. There is the cat which is inferior only in respect to its type and color—not in relation to its basic structure and health.

There is then the inferior cat produced by those who are in Siamese just to make money. These people have cats that they breed with no consideration for the vigor of the offspring. Such kittens are invariably sickly and prone to illnesses throughout their lives. Poor health and inferior Siamese result from unplanned matings and excessive breeding, coupled with a lack of ongoing selection being applied to future breeding stock.

How do you make the right choice when selecting a Siamese? The answer is you do your homework. Visit shows, talk to established exhibitors, and judges. When you visit the seller take a good look at his stock, and more especially the living conditions of the cats. Is he giving you the hard sell, or does he seem more concerned about the kitten's future home? Sometimes the dedicated seller might even annoy you, but he is concerned for his kittens, even if they are not quality Siamese. The more Siamese you see, the more likely you are to make a wise choice.

WHICH SEX TO PURCHASE?

From the viewpoint of pet suitability, there really is no difference between a tom (male) and a queen (female). Some people prefer one sex, but this is purely subjective. This author has found males to be more consistent in their character than females, who may tend to be "all or nothing" in their attitude. In other words, they can be extremely affectionate one day, but rather standoffish the next. The tom

There is a cornucopia of average Siamese cats, but only a few emerge as show quality. If you are looking for a high standard cat, it will be a costly purchase.

tends to be much the same from one day to the next, whatever his character might be.

It really is a pot-luck matter just how affectionate a kitten will grow up to become. Cats are very much individuals, and they can change as they grow up. The way they are treated also affects their personality. Therefore, it is more a case of selecting a kitten that appeals to you, regardless of its sex.

Of course, if you wish to become a breeder then the female has to be the better choice. Once she reaches breeding age you can then select a suitable mate for her from the hundreds of quality stud males available to you. If you purchase a male with the view to owning a stud, you are really gambling that he will mature into a fine cat that others would want to use. For this to happen, your tom would need to be very successful in the show ring, and then in the quality of his offspring.

Furthermore, owning a whole tom (a male that has not been neutered) does present more practical problems than owning a queen. Such a male will be continually marking his territory (your furniture) by spraying it with his urine, which is hardly a fragrant scent!

If your Siamese is to be a pet only, then regardless of the sex you should have it neutered or spayed. It will be more affectionate to you, will not be wandering off looking for romance, and will not shed its coat as excessively as would an unaltered Siamese. In the case of a tom, he will not come home with pieces of his ears missing as a result of his fights with other entire males. Your queen will not present you with kittens that you do not want but which she will have if she is not spayed. She is far less likely to spray than is the male, but she will show her desire to mate, both with her "calling" sounds, which can be eerie, and her provocative crouching position in which she is clearly inviting a mating.

WHAT AGE TO PURCHASE?

Breeders vary in the age they judge a kitten ready for a new home. An important consideration is obviously if the new owners have experience of cats generally and kittens in particular. While an eight-week-old baby is quite delightful, it is invariably better from a health standpoint that the kitten remains with its mother until it is ten or more weeks of age. Some breeders will not part with a kitten until it is 16 weeks of age.

The kitten should have received at least temporary vaccinations against feline distemper and rabies (if applicable in your country and if the kitten is over 12 weeks of age) and preferably protection against other major feline infections. Additionally, you should let your own vet examine your Siamese.

Although most owners will wish to obtain a kitten, a potential breeder or exhibitor may find that a young adult (over eight to nine months of age) is more suitable to

Generally, it is hard to get a kitten from a breeder before it is 10 weeks of age, and some won't give them up until 16 weeks of age.

his needs. By this age the quality of the Siamese is becoming more apparent. However, bear in mind that a mature Siamese queen will not be at her peak until she is about two years of age. A tom will be even later in reaching full maturity, and he may not peak until he is five years of age.

ONE OR TWO SIAMESE?

Without any doubt, two kittens are always preferred to one. They provide constant company for each other and are a delight to watch as they play. The extra costs involved in their upkeep are unlikely to be a factor if you are able to afford a Siamese in the first place.

Above: Getting two Siamese kittens instead of one allows them to have playmates and may spare you from having to deal with a bored or destructive housemate.

Below: Before selecting a Siamese, it is always wise to do your homework. Make sure the cat has health clearances and has been reared with kind handling.

Age is a consideration when choosing your cat. If you can't be around all the time, getting an adult Siamese may be better than getting a kitten.

GENERAL CARE & GROOMING

Siamese cats are extremely easy to cater to in terms of their accommodation and general care. This chapter will discuss purchasing the essential and nonessential accessories for your cat, socializing your cat with children and other animals, making a safe environment for your cat, and disciplining your cat the proper and most effective way.

ESSENTIAL ACCESSORIES

Litter Tray

Every cat will need a litter tray so that it can relieve itself whenever it wishes to. If this is not provided from the outset, the only possible consequence is that the cat will be forced to foul your carpet or some other surface. There are many styles and sizes of litter trays, and the larger ones are the best for long term service. Some have igloo-type hoods, both to provide a sense of privacy for the cat and to retain any odors. However, an open tray is just as good and will not in any case be foul smelling if it is cleaned as it should be.

You will need to purchase cat litter for the base of the tray. There are many brands to choose from, and some have odor neutralizers already in them. Cover the base with enough litter to absorb urine and for the cat to scratch around in. In the event you should run out of litter, you can use coarse grade sawdust or wood shavings. These are preferred to garden soil because the latter may contain the eggs of parasitic worms or other parasites.

The tray should be cleaned after each use, removing that which is soiled. A small dustpan is handy for attending to this chore. Once a week, you should disinfect and thoroughly rinse the tray. Place the tray near the kitchen door. Once a cat is an adult, it will rarely use its tray if it has access to a garden. However, in the winter months, it may start to use it because many cats do not like to go out if it is wet or if there is a deep snow covering.

Housetraining is easily accomplished with a kitten. When you see it searching for somewhere to relieve itself, which will be accompanied by crying, it should be gently lifted and placed into its tray. Never scold a kitten for fouling the floor, it will not understand why you are annoyed with it. You must watch the kitten after it has played and after it wakes up because these are prime times for it to want to relieve itself. Remember, kittens cannot control their bowel movements for more than a few seconds; this time increases considerably as the cat matures. If you exhibit patience, you will find the kitty quickly gets to know what is expected of it. Cats are fastidious

When you get your Siamese kitten home, it is going to need the essentials, like a litter box, collar, and maybe even a bed.

Scratching posts offer hours of healthy exercise and enjoyment for cats and kittens while preventing them from damaging the furniture. Photo courtesy of Cosmic Pet Products.

about cleanliness, so if they foul the home, there is invariably a reason for so doing. Often it will be because the litter tray has not been cleaned or you were not around enough when the cat was a kitten.

Scratching Post

Here again there are many styles to choose from. All have a fabric on them, and the post may be free standing or the sort that is screwed to a wall. You can also purchase carpet-clad climbing frames, which are more expensive but greatly enjoyed by cats. When you see your kitten or cat go to scratch your armchair, lift it up and place it against the scratching post. Gently draw its front feet down the post a few times. Again, if this is repeated a number of times, the kitten will understand that it can claw away on the post but not on the furniture. As it grows older, it will no doubt test your resolve now and then, but usually if you clap your hands and say, "No," in a firm voice, it will realize you are keeping an eye on it!

Cat Collar

All cats should wear a cat collar fitted with an identity disc. In many cities, this is a law. The collar may be of the elasticized type or not. Be sure it is neither too tight nor loose. You should be able to place a finger between the collar and the cat's neck.

Carry Box

The carry box is so useful that I regard it as an essential item for all cat owners. It will be needed when you visit the vet, when traveling, or when you need to contain the cat for any reason. It also makes a fine bed for a kitten. The box can be made of wicker, wood, wire, or fiberglass. The latter are probably the best but can be expensive if they are of a high quality. It is essential that they should be large enough for the adult cat to stand upright in and not be forced to stoop. Be sure the box has adequate ventilation and can be securely closed.

Female seal point kitten.

The base of the box can be fitted with a good lining of newspaper on which a blanket is placed. A kitten will find this a nice bed, especially if it has a companion. If not, place a cuddly toy in with it to snuggle up against. When it is a kitten and during its first week or so in its new home, it is better that it is confined at night, so it cannot harm itself by wandering about the home. Once it is totally familiar with your home, you can leave the carry-box door open at night so it can come and go as it wishes.

Feeding Dishes

You will want one dish for moist cat food, one for biscuit food, and one for water. You can purchase dishes made of earthenware, aluminum, stainless steel, or plastic. You can also use saucers or any combination of these. The main thing is that they are kept spotlessly clean, so they should be washed after each use. The water dish should be cleaned and replenished each day.

Brush

Cats do not come any simpler to groom than a Siamese. Even so, your cat should have its own brush, preferably of a medium-bristle type. A chamois leather or silk cloth is also useful to give your cat that extra sheen after it has been brushed. Although the Siamese hardly needs any brushing, it is useful to attend to this once a week. This makes your cat familiar with being handled, and at such a time, you can give

it a check over. Inspect its ears to see that they are free of wax and check the teeth to see that they are clean. Inspect the pads to ensure that they are firm but supple. Part the toes with your fingers just to make sure they are free of debris. Lodged in the skin, dirt and grass could be the source of an abscess if they are not removed. Gently feel the abdomen to check that there are no swellings.

NON ESSENTIAL ACCESSORIES

Basket or Bed

If you obtain a carry box for your kitten, then a bed is not a necessity. If your Siamese becomes like most other cats, it will probably not use its basket/bed—even though it cost you a bundle! Cats like to choose their own place to sleep, and indeed they will have numerous places depending on their mood, the ambient temperature, and who happens to be in your home at a given time. Some will have a favorite chair or sofa, some may prefer a secluded spot behind a chair, while others will prefer to sleep on your bed, knowing this to be a warm and popular place with their "human-cat" companions.

Better than a conventional basket would be to invest in one of the many carpet-clad, wooden furniture pieces produced these days for cats. These are fun and take into account the cat's preference for sleeping above floor level. Some cats do sleep in baskets, so it is a case of reviewing all the options and

Loving your Siamese cat begins with proper care. Be sure to give your Siamese the essentials and spend lots of time playing and petting.

deciding which you think will best meet your needs.

Cat Door

The cat door or flap allows your feline friends to go out onto your enclosed porch. Alternatively, you can adjust the door to open only one way. Apart from manually opening cat doors, you can also purchase silent electronic doors!

Halter or Harness

If you plan on taking your cat with you on holidays or generally when you travel, it will be found that a cat collar does not offer you full control over your Siamese. Additionally to the collar, you could purchase one of the numerous halters now available for cats. Choose one that fits snugly. Those with top fastenings are easy to place on your cat. Do not obtain dog harnesses because they will be too big around the chest, even if they are for small dogs.

Lead training is best done while your pet is young. Place the halter on the kitten and let it become familiar with it before you attempt to attach the lead. When the halter does not bother the cat, you can then attach the lead and let the cat wander about in the privacy of your yard. Here it will become used to the fact that there is a restraint on its movements. The process cannot be hurried because cats do not like to be restricted. Devote only a few minutes per day to lead training and always encourage the cat with plenty of physical reward.

Do not take the cat from the confines of its home territory until it is really relaxed on a lead. In the event of a dog suddenly appearing, the halter allows you to maintain control of the cat, which should be promptly lifted up. If it is not your intention to take your cat on regular outings, there is little point in lead training it because cats are generally not happy away from their home range.

Toys

There is no shortage of commercially made cat toys these days. Avoid soft, plastic ones that your pet might break apart and swallow pieces from. Simple things, such as bobbins on a string or bits of cloth attached to a springy cable, will also amuse your Siamese. If you devote time to playing with your cats, you will find that they will learn how to play games with you, and it will strengthen the bond between you and your cat.

CATS & CHILDREN

If there are young children in your home, it is most important that they are taught from the outset to respect your new kitten or cat. Children must understand that cats should not be disturbed if they are sleeping and should not be handled in an incorrect manner. When being lifted, a cat should never be grasped by the loose fur on its neck. Always support the full body weight with one hand, while securing the cat firmly but gently around the neck with the other hand.

Children should be made aware of the fact that even kittens can inflict a nasty scratch on them if the kitten is not treated with kindness and consideration. Essentially, you must always be watchful if young

Good grooming should start at an early age. Your pet shop can help you select the proper grooming aids for your cat. Photo courtesy of The Kong Company.

children are playing with the family cat until they are old enough to understand how it must be handled.

CATS & OTHER PETS

The cat is a prime predator and should not be left in the company of young rabbits, guinea pigs, hamsters, or mice if these other pets are out of their cage. As a general rule, if a pet is as big as your cat or is another carnivore, it will usually be safe. Cats and dogs get on really well if they are brought up together. However, if a kitten is introduced into a home that has an adult dog, due care must be exercised. The first thing to ensure is that the resident pet gets extra attention so it does not become jealous of the new arrival.

The kitten and other pets must come to terms with each other in their own time and manner — it is not something you can hurry. In some instances, a newly acquired cat may make friends very quickly with dogs or other household cats. In other cases, the best that ever happens is a sort of truce, each accepting the other but avoiding contact most of the time. Kittens will invariably be accepted much more readily than will adult cats. The latter, of course, will have developed their own attitudes to other animals depending on what their experiences have been with them.

SAFEGUARDING A KITTEN

When a kitten is first introduced to your home, there are many potential dangers that it must be protected from. For example, a door left ajar on a windy day could easily slam shut on the kitty. An unprotected balcony is an obvious danger to a young feline, as is a garden pond. An open fire is yet another example of how a kitten might easily become injured. They are, of course, naturally cautious of dangerous situations, but even so, it is best to watch out for them just as their mother would.

The kitchen is probably the most dangerous place for kittens. A typical scenario is that you might turn around from the stove with a pan of boiling water or a kettle in your hand, only to trip over the kitten. The water may scald the kitten or yourself badly, and the fall would not do you any good either! Kittens just love to pounce and hang onto string and its like. The latter might be the cord from an electric iron you are using— the result being obvious. As your Siamese gets a little older, it will easily be able to jump onto kitchen units and should be educated at an early age not to do this in this particular room.

The other important area of safeguarding a kitten is in relation to ensuring it is given maximum

protection against major feline diseases. This is done via vaccinations. Consult your vet about these as soon as you have obtained your Siamese. Do not allow the kitten out of the house until it has complete protection.

DISCIPLINE

Cats are very intelligent and respond to discipline just as dogs and most other comparable pets will. They are not dangerous to people so do not need the level of training that a dog does to fit into a human world. It's really a case in which your cat should understand one simple command— "no". Its name given in a firm voice, which convey the same information. If it goes to

Siamese count among the most curious and inventive of all cats—this young fellow wants to see the world.

scratch the furniture, you should promptly lift it up and say, "No." A very light tap on its rump will enforce the command. This is about the extent of discipline that will ever be needed.

The most important thing you must remember whether training a cat, a dog, a horse, or a large

Showing off its alert personality and good balance is Ch. Blakthai's Victoria, owned by Virginia Blackwood.

parrot, is that they relate only to the moment. The longer the time lapse between the act and discipline, the less chance there is that the animal will associate one action with another. You can work on the basis that if you are unable to administer discipline within seconds of an unwanted act, you may as well not bother. If the kitten or cat is out of distance, clapping your hands at the same time as saying the command can be effective. Alternatively, you might be able to throw some light object at the cat at the same time as the command is given.

All animal training is based on the fact that the animal associates a given action with a given response. The latter will either be neutral (i.e. nothing happens), positive, or negative. Neither cats nor dogs will understand a lengthy lecture, but they will rapidly understand instant responses to their own actions. You will thus use both positive and negative "enforcers" in training your cat. If your Siamese meows for some food or to go out and you respond promptly, this will enforce the action that will be repeated at a later date. The more you respond, the greater will be implantation of that action in the cat. The same goes for discipline.

You should never need to use forcible discipline with a cat. If you think carefully about any given action and apply an appropriate response fairly and consistently (the latter being crucial), you will develop a real understanding with your feline friend.

Siamese kittens are naturally clean—most kittens arrive to their new homes fully litter trained.

FEEDING YOUR SIAMESE

Cats and kittens are very much like people when it comes to their eating habits. Some are extremely easy to satisfy; others are much more difficult to please. Adult cats can be a worry, but at least you know they must have eaten something to have survived to maturity. Kittens, on the other hand, can prematurely turn your hair gray because you fear they may not thrive unless you can come up with some delicacy that tempts their palate!

Fortunately, there are so many quality brands of commercial cat foods available today that it should be possible to get even the most fastidious of kittens through its most difficult early months.

CATS ARE CARNIVORES

The cat is a prime predator in its wild habitat, and this means its basic diet must be composed of the flesh of other animals, be they mammals, birds, or fish. The digestive tract of a carnivore has evolved to cope with proteins, but it has little ability to digest raw vegetable matter. This means the latter must first be boiled, so that the hard cellulose walls of such foods are softened, then broken down by the digestive juices and flora found in the alimentary tract.

In the wild, the cat would eat just about every part of its prey, leaving only the bones that were too large for it to digest. This diet would provide proteins and fats from the body tissues, roughage from the fur or feathers, and carbohydrates and vitamins from the partially digested vegetable matter that would be in the intestines of the prey. Combined with water, a very well-balanced diet would be provided for the cat. An equivalent of such nutrition is what you must strive to supply.

COMMERCIAL FOODS

The range of commercial cat foods encompasses canned, semi-moist, and dry diets. We have always found that our cats have never really enjoyed any of the semi-moist foods. The canned and dry foods come in an extensive range of flavors, which include meat, fish, and poultry. Of the canned foods, some have a firm consistency; others are chunks in a sauce. There are also formulated kitten foods.

Commercial foods can form the basis of your Siamese's diet, but you should supply a variety of them to reduce the chances that some key constituent is missing from the diet. Siamese will no doubt help in this matter because they seem to tire of one brand if it is fed daily. Indeed, deciding which is their chosen flavor of the week can be an interesting guessing game. They will suddenly show no interest in a product they seemed to eat with relish just a few days earlier! You will find that some cats enjoy fish flavors, others poultry and yet others, the various meats.

Dry food is enjoyed by most, though not all, Siamese. It provides good exercise for the teeth and jaw muscles, which canned foods do not. Their other advantage is that you can leave them out all day without their losing their appeal to your pets, or attracting flies. Water must always be available to your cats;

it is best to stay with white fish such as cod. Tuna, sardines, and other canned fish are appreciated, but give only small quantities of them as a treat because they may prove too rich for your pet's system. Chicken is enjoyed by nearly all cats.

Cheese, egg yolk, spaghetti, and even boiled rice are all items that you can offer to your pets to see if it appeals to them. Small beef and other meat bones that still have

Commercial cat foods are fortified with essential vitamins and minerals. They are available in dry, moist, and semi-moist varieties. Photo courtesy of Drs. Arthur and Judy Topilow.

this is even more important if the basic diet is of dried foods.

NON-COMMERCIAL FOODS

Your Siamese will enjoy many of the foods that you eat. These foods provide both variety and good exercise for the jaws. Human consumption meats can be of beef, pork, or lamb. All fish should be steamed or boiled, and

some meat on them will be enjoyed and keep a kitten or cat amused for quite some time. Beware of bones that easily splinter, such as those of chicken or rabbit.

You can by all means see if small pieces of vegetables or fruits are accepted if mixed with the food, but generally cats will leave them. This is no problem

Giving your Siamese cat a bone with some meat still on it will be enjoyed by your cat, but be careful that the bone isn't too small or your cat may choke on it — this bone isn't a problem!

providing that the cat is receiving commercial foods as its basic diet. Such products are all fortified with essential vitamins after the cooking process.

HOW MUCH TO FEED?

Cats prefer to eat a little but often, rather than consume one mighty meal a day. However, as carnivores, adults are well able to cope with one large meal a day. The same is not true of kittens, which should receive three or four meals per day. A kitten or a cat will normally only consume that which is needed. You can arrive at this amount by trial and error. If kitty devours its meal and is looking for more, then let it have more. You will quickly be able to judge how much each kitten needs to satisfy itself. Always remove any moist foods that are uneaten after each meal.

At 12 weeks of age the kitten should have four meals a day. One of these meals can be omitted when the kitten is 16 weeks old, but increase the quantity of the other three. You can reduce to two meals a day when the kitten is about nine months of age. From that age, it is best to continue feeding two meals—one in the morning and one in the early evening. How many times a day you feed your adult cat is unimportant. The key factor is that it receives as much as it needs over the day, and that the diet is balanced to provide the essential ingredients discussed earlier. It is also better that meals are given regularly. Cats, like humans, are creatures of habit.

Treats can be provided on an occasional basis to help provide a little variety in the diet. Some treats act as a cleansing agent to help reduce tartar on the cat's teeth. Photo courtesy of Heinz.

WATER

If a cat's diet is essentially of moist foods, it will drink far less than if the diet is basicaliy of dry foods. Many cats do not like faucet (tap) water because they are able to smell and taste the many additives included by your local water board. Chlorine is high on this list. Although it dissipates into the air quite readily, chloromides do not, which is why the cat may ignore the water. During the filtering process at the water station, chemicals are both taken out and added. The resulting mineral balance and

Although your Siamese may prefer many smaller meals through the day, never leave wet food out for extended periods.

taste is often not to a cat's liking. This is why you will see cats drinking from puddles, a flower vase, or even your toilet, because the taste is better for them. If your water is refused, then you can see if your cat prefers mineralized bottled water—not distilled because the latter has no mineral content to it.

THE NEW ARRIVAL

It is a very traumatic time for a kitten when it leaves its mother and siblings. It will often eat well the first day; however, as it starts to miss its family, it will fret. You can reduce its stress by providing the diet it was receiving from the seller. You can change the diet slowly, if necessary, as it settles down. Of course, many kittens have no problems, but if yours does, this feeding advice should help its period of adjustment.

What is essential is that the kitten takes in sufficient liquids so that it does not start to dehydrate. This, more than anything else, will adversely affect its health very rapidly. If you are at all concerned, do consult your vet. The kitten may have picked up a virus, but if it is treated promptly, this should not be a problem. Your vet might supply you with a dietary supplement, which we have found excellent for kittens experiencing "new home syndrome."

KEEPING YOUR SIAMESE HEALTHY

Like any other animal, your Siamese can fall victim to hundreds of diseases and conditions. Most can be prevented by sound husbandry. The majority, should they be recognized in their early stages, can be treated with modern drugs or by surgery. Clearly, preventive techniques are better and less costly than treatments, yet in many instances a cat will become ill because the owner has neglected some basic aspect of general management. In this chapter, we are not so much concerned with cataloging all the diseases your cat could contract, because these are legion, but more concerned with reviewing sound management methods.

HYGIENE

Always apply routine hygiene to all aspects of your pet's management. This alone dramatically reduces the chances of your pet becoming ill because it restricts pathogens (disease-causing organisms) from building up colonies that are able to overcome the natural defense mechanisms of your Siamese.

Inspecting and cleaning your Siamese's ears are important in keeping them free of parasites and wax buildup.

1. After your cat has eaten its fill of any moist foods, either discard the food or keep it for later by placing it in your refrigerator. Anything left uneaten at the end of the day can be trashed. Always wash the bowl after each meal. Do not feed your pet from any dishes that are chipped, cracked, or, in the case of plastic, those that are badly scratched.

2. Always store food in a dry, cool cupboard or in the refrigerator in the case of fresh foods.

3. For whatever reason, if you have been handling someone else's cats, always wash your hands before handling your own cats.

4. Be rigorous in cleaning your cat's litter box as soon as you see that it has been fouled.

5. Pay particular attention to the grooming of a Siamese cat because so many problems can begin with a seemingly innocuous event. For example, in itself, a minor cut may not be a major problem as long as it is treated with an antiseptic. But if it is left as an open untreated wound, it is an obvious site for bacterial colonization. The bacteria then gain access to the bloodstream, and a major problem ensues that might not even be associated with the initial wound. The same applies to flea or lice bites. Inspect the skin carefully for signs of flea droppings when you groom a Siamese. These appear like minute specks of black dust.

Trimming your Siamese's nails will keep them from getting caught on things such as your rugs, blankets, clothes, and furniture.

RECOGNIZING AN ILL CAT

You must be able to recognize when your cat is ill in order to seek a solution to the problem. You must learn to distinguish between a purely temporary condition and that which will need some form of veterinary advice and/or treatment. For example, a cat can sprain a muscle by jumping and landing awkwardly. This would normally correct itself over a 36-48 hour period. Your pet may contract a slight chill, or its feces might become loose. Both conditions will normally correct themselves over a day or so. On the other hand, if a condition persists for more than two days, it would be advisable to telephone your vet for advice.

In general, any appearance or behavior that is not normal for your cat would suggest something is responsible for the abnormality. This is your first indication that something may be amiss. The following are a number of signs that indicate a problem:

1. Diarrhea, especially if it is very liquid, foul-smelling or blood-streaked. If blood is seen in the urine, this is also an indication of a problem, as is excessive straining or cries of pain when the cat tries to relieve itself.

2. Discharge from the nose or eyes, if excessive, needs veterinary attention. This may be due to blocked tear ducts.

3. Repeated vomiting. All cats are sick occasionally with indigestion. They will also vomit after eating grass, but repeated vomiting is not normal.

4. Wheezing sounds when breathing, or any other suggestion of breathing difficulties.

5. Excessive scratching. All cats will have a good scratch on a quite regular basis, but excessive scratching indicates a skin problem, especially if it has created sores or lesions.

6. Constant rubbing of the rear end along the ground.

7. Bald patches, lesions, cuts, and swellings on the body, legs, tail, or face.

8. The coat seems to lack bounce or life, and is dull.

9. The cat is listless and lethargic, showing little interest in what is going on around it.

10. The eyes have a glazed look to them, or the haw (nictitating membrane, or third eyelid) is clearly visible.

11. The cat is displaying an unusual lack of interest in its favorite food items.

12. The gums of the teeth seem very red or swollen.

13. Fits or other abnormal signs of behavior.

14. Any obvious pain or distress.

Very often two or more clinical signs will be apparent when a condition is developing. The number of signs increases as the disease or ailment advances to a more sinister stage.

DIAGNOSIS

Correct diagnosis is of the utmost importance before any form of treatment can be administered. Often it will require blood and/or fecal microscopy in order to establish the exact cause of a condition. Many of the signs listed above are common to most diseases, so never attempt home diagnosis and treatment: if you are wrong, your cherished Siamese may pay for your error with its life. Once ill health is suspected, any lost time favors the pathogens and makes treatment both more difficult and more costly.

In making your original decision to purchase a Siamese, or any other cat, you should always have allowed for the cost of veterinary treatment. If this is likely to be a burden that you cannot afford, then do not purchase a cat. The first few months, and especially the first weeks, is the time when most cats will become ill. If they survive this period, the chances are that future visits to the vet will be rare, other than for booster vaccinations.

Kittens do not have the immunity to pathogens that the adult cat does, nor do they have the muscle reserves of the adult. If they are ill, they need veterinary help very quickly if they are to have a good chance of overcoming a disease or major problem.

Having decided that your cat is not well, you should make notes on paper of the signs of the problem, when you first noticed them, and how quickly things have deteriorated. If possible, obtain a fecal and urine sample, then telephone your vet and make an appointment. Ask other cat owners in your area who their vet is. Some vets display a greater liking for cats, or dogs, or horses than do others. This is just human nature, but obviously you want to go to one that has a special affection for felines.

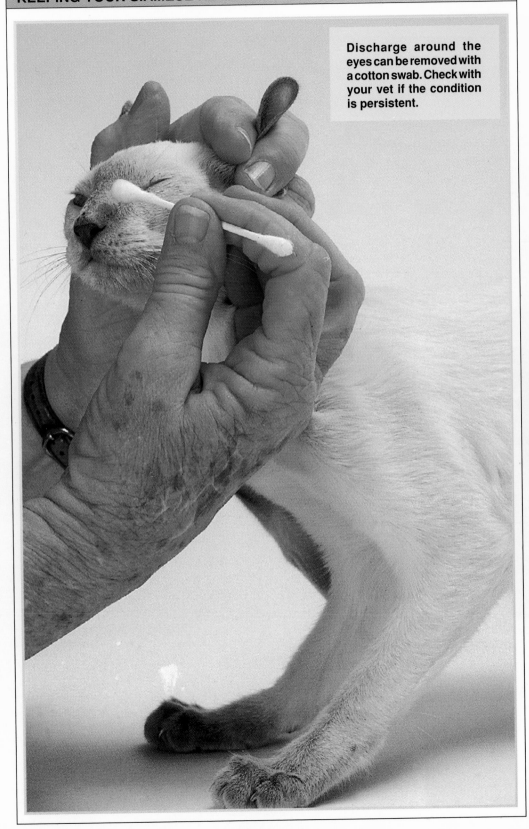

Discharge around the eyes can be removed with a cotton swab. Check with your vet if the condition is persistent.

TREATMENT

Once your vet has prescribed a course of treatment, it is important that you follow it exactly as instructed. Do not discontinue the medicine because the cat shows a big improvement. Such an action could prove counterproductive, and the pathogens that had not been killed might develop an immunity to the treatment. A relapse could occur, and this might be more difficult to deal with.

VACCINATIONS

There are a few extremely dangerous diseases that afflict cats, but fortunately there are vaccines that can dramatically reduce the risk of them infecting your Siamese. The bacteria and viruses that cause such diseases are often found in the air wherever there are cats. Discuss a program of immunization with your vet.

When a kitten is born, it inherits protection from disease via the colostrum of its mother's milk. Such protection may last for up to 16 weeks—but it varies from kitten to kitten and may last only six weeks. It is therefore recommended that your kitten be vaccinated against diseases at six to eight weeks of age just to be on the safe side. Boosters are required some weeks later and thereafter each year. Potential breeding females should be given boosters about three to four weeks prior to the due date. This will ensure that a high level of antibodies is passed to the kittens.

An important consideration with regard to the major killer diseases in cats is the treatment of infection. If a cat survives an infection, it will probably be a carrier of the disease and shed the pathogens continually throughout its life. The only safe course is therefore to ensure that your kittens are protected. The main diseases for which there are vaccinations are as follows:

Rabies: This is a disease of the neurological system. It is non-existent in Great Britain, Ireland, Australia, New Zealand, Hawaii, certain oceanic islands, Holland, Sweden, and Norway. In these countries, extremely rigid quarantine laws are applied to ensure it stays that way. You cannot have your cat vaccinated against rabies if you live in one of these countries, unless you are about to emigrate with your cat. In all other countries, rabies vaccinations are either compulsory or strongly advised. They are given when the kitten is three or more months of age.

Feline panleukopenia: Also known as feline infectious enteritis, and feline distemper. This is a highly contagious viral disease. Vaccinations are given when the kitten is about eight weeks old, and a booster is given four weeks later. In high-risk areas, a third injection may be advised four weeks after the second one.

Feline respiratory disease complex: Often referred to as cat flu but this is incorrect. Although a number of diseases are within this group, two of them are

Some feline diseases are communicable from cat to cat—keep your feline friend current on all necessary vaccinations.

especially dangerous. They are feline viral rhinotracheitis (FVR) and feline calicivirus (FCV). The vaccination for the prevention of these diseases is combined and given when the kitten is six or more weeks of age; a booster follows three to four weeks later.

Feline leukemia virus complex (FeLV): This disease was first recognized in 1964, and a vaccine became available in the US in about 1985. Like "cat flu," the name is misleading, because it is far more complex than a blood cancer, which is what its name implies. Essentially, it destroys the cat's immune system, so the cat may contract any of the major diseases.

The disease is easily spread via the saliva of a cat as it licks other cats. It is also spread prenatally from an infected queen to her offspring via the blood, or when washing her kittens. This is why it is important to test all breeding cats for FeLV. Vaccination is worthwhile only on a kitten or cat that has tested negative. If a cat tests positive for the disease, it has a 70 percent chance of survival, though it will be a carrier in many instances.

Feline infectious peritonitis (FIP): This disease has various effects on the body's metabolism. There are no satisfactory tests for it, but intranasal liquid vaccinations via a dropper greatly reduce the potential for it to develop in the tissues of the nose.

PARASITES

Parasites are organisms that live on or in a host. They feed from it without providing any benefit in return. External parasites include fleas, lice, ticks, flies, and any other creature that

Allowing your Siamese outdoors makes him more suseptible to fleas, ticks, and other parasites. Your Siamese is safer kept in your home.

Owning more than one cat increases your responsibility to maintain good husbandry practices.

bites the skin of the cat. Internal parasites include all pathogens, but the term is more commonly applied to worms in their various forms.

External parasites and their eggs can be seen with the naked eye. All can be eradicated with treatment from your vet. However, initial treatment will need to be followed by further treatments because most compounds are ineffective on the eggs. The repeat treatments kill the larvae as they hatch. It is also important that all bedding be treated or destroyed because this is often where parasites prefer to live when not on the host.

All cats are host to a range of worm species. If worms multiply in the cat, they adversely affect its health. They will cause loss of appetite, wasting, and a steady deterioration in health. At a high level of infestation, they may be seen in the fecal matter, but normally it will require fecal microscopy by your vet. This will establish the species and the relative density of the eggs, thus the level of infestation.

Treatment is normally via tablets, but liquids are also available. Because worms are so common, the best husbandry technique is to routinely treat breeding cats for worms prior to their being bred, then for the queen and her kittens to be treated periodically. Discuss a testing and treatment program with your vet.

NEUTERING AND SPAYING

Desexing your cat is normally done when a female is about four months of age and somewhat later with a male. The operation is quite simple with a male but more complicated with a female. It is still a routine procedure. It is possible to delay estrus in a breeding queen, but the risk of negative side effects makes this a dubious course to take. Discuss it with your vet. A cat of any age can be neutered (male) or spayed (female); but if they are adults, they take some months (especially males) before they lose their old habits.

FIRST AID

Although you might think that such inquisitive creatures as cats would be prone to many physical injuries, this is not actually the case. They usually extricate themselves from dangerous situations because of their very fast reflexes. However, injuries do happen, and the most common is caused by the cat darting across a road and being hit by a vehicle. About 40 percent of cats die annually due to traffic accidents. The next level of injury will be caused by cats getting bitten or scratched when fighting among themselves, or being bitten by an insect, or by a sharp object getting lodged in their fur or feet.

If your cat is hit by a vehicle, the first thing to do is to try and place it on a board of some sort and remove it to a safe place. Do not lift its head because this might result in it swallowing blood into the lungs. Try to keep it calm by talking soothingly to it.

If the cat is still mobile, but has clearly been badly hurt, you must try and restrict its movements by wrapping it in a blanket or towel. If it is bleeding badly, try to contain the flow by wrapping a bandage around the body or leg to reduce the blood loss. With a minor cut, you should trim the hair away from the wound, bathe it, then apply an antiseptic or stem the flow with a styptic pencil or other coagulant.

If you suspect that your cat has been bitten by an insect and the result is a swelling, the poison is already in the skin so external ointments will have virtually no effect. The same is true of an abscess caused by fighting. The only answer is to let your vet use surgery to lance and treat the wound.

Fortunately, cats rarely swallow poison because they are such careful eaters. In all instances, immediately contact your vet and advise him of the kind of poison the cat has consumed.

If your cat should ever be badly frightened, for example, by a dog chasing and maybe biting it, the effect of this may not be apparent immediately. It may go into shock some time later. Keep the cat indoors so that you can see how it reacts. Should it go into shock and collapse, place a blanket around it and take it to the vet. If this is not possible, place it in a darkened room and cover it with a blanket so it does not lose too much body heat. Comfort it until you can make contact with the vet.

This bright-eyed, alert Siamese is the picture of good health.

SIAMESE COLORS & STANDARD

To the first-time Siamese owner, the way in which colors and patterns are perceived by the various cat registration bodies can seem a little confusing. An explanation of the classification of the Siamese will hopefully make the situation more clear. The original Siamese had a dark brown face and ears and dark brown on the legs and tail. This contrasted against a lighter colored body. The brown coloration was termed *seal point*.

As time passed by, a lighter colored brown was developed called *chocolate point*. It was created by a gene that diluted the seal color. A *blue point* was also developed, and with the added dilution gene created, the *lilac point* emerged (also know as *frost* in the USA). These became the four classic Siamese colors and were derived without going outside of the Siamese breed.

The next stage in developments was that Siamese were crossed with other breeds in order to introduce further colors, such as red and its dilution, cream. These in turn enabled the *tortie point* to be derived. The *tabby point* completed the possibilities, and both tortie and tabby were produced in various shades, such as blue-tabby point and blue-tortie point. The emergence of these many variations created quite a stir in the breed, with people being divided into two

basic camps. There were the purists who claimed that the non-basic colored Siamese should not be called Siamese because their color was the result of hybridization. Then there were those that argued these new colors were still Siamese because a number of generations of breeding back to the Siamese had removed virtually all of the genes from the outcross breeds (usually domestic shorthairs).

The result of these arguments eventually resulted in two situations. In Great Britain, the additional colors were accepted during the 1960s as being color varieties of the Siamese. In the USA, the largest registration body, the Cat Fanciers Association (CFA) regarded any non-original colors as being a separate breed. They called it the Colorpoint Shorthair, and do so to this day. Other American associations have largely followed the UK stance and accept all other colors as being Siamese.

In other words, if you live in Great Britain, then all the many color variations seen in the Siamese are accepted as being of that breed. If you live in the USA and register your cat with the CFA, then only the four basic colors are accepted as Siamese (seal, chocolate, blue, and lilac points), and all others are a separate breed called the Colorpoint Shorthair. If you register with associations such as the American Cat Association, the Cat Fanciers Federation, or most others, all of the numerous colors are accepted as Siamese. The latter situation also prevails throughout Europe and in Australia and Canada.

To complete the story about Siamese colors, you can also see what appears to be self (single) colored Siamese. These are, however, a separate breed called either Oriental or Foreign shorthaired. They were also developed by hybridization, but because they do not exhibit the Siamese pattern, they are thus not Siamese, even though their appearance is just the same.

THE SIAMESE PATTERN

Before describing the various Siamese colors, you may be interested in knowing about an unusual aspect of this pattern called thermo-sensitive, which means the density of the color is affected by the ambient temperature the cat lives in. The effect of the genetic mutation that creates the Siamese pattern is that it does not allow pigment to form on the body as it does at the extremities (the face, ears, legs, and tail). Each of these is just slightly cooler than is the rest of the body.

When a Siamese kitten is born, it is retained in a very warm environment close to its mother. As a result, the Siamese pattern is not evident but begins to show itself after a few days. While all Siamese and numerous other species, such as rabbits, mice, and cavies, that display the "Himalayan" pattern are all thermo-sensitive, there is some variation in the effect of the temperature between individuals. It is not that at a given temperature the density of the pigment fades, but is more a case of at what temperature the gene triggers the pigment to fade. This means that kittens in the same litter can vary in the way temperature affects their color. At a given heat, one cat may not be affected needing a slightly higher temperature to cause the pigment to lighten. A second factor called gene modifiers, which can be selected by the breeder, is also involved because some cats have a more dense pigment to start with. Yet another factor that may alter the perceived shade of the pigment is that of direct sunlight, which will of course bleach any color.

THE SIAMESE COLORS

Eyes

In all instances, the breed must have blue eyes. The terms used to describe these include: clear, brilliant, deep blue, clear-vivid blue, bright-intense blue, and deep-vivid blue. The actual creation of the blue in a cat's eyes is the result of what is known as *Tyndall's phenomenon*. The eye acts as a prism in splitting up light waves and reflecting white light. No yellow-brown pigment is formed in the pupil of a Siamese. A thin layer of black melanin absorbs all long light waves, but the shorter ones, which are blue, are reflected back.

Seal point Siamese are the most common of all the different color points of the Siamese cat breed.

Body

The body should be the specified color that shades, if at all, imperceptibly into a lighter color on the belly. There is a considerable range of body colors seen in the breed. In some instances, the desired color is as it should be—even and with no shading. In other examples, there is obvious shading seen, sometimes on the back, and in others more on the rear end of the cat than on the front part.

Points

Mask, ears, legs, feet, and tail should all exhibit the required color. This should match on all points and should show clear contrast between the points and the body color. There should also be areas of lighter color on the forehead, rather than a complete hood of the points colors. The facial points should connect to the ears by what are termed tracings, which are variable amounts of the points color, and the mask should not extend onto the neck.

Faults

Incorrect eye color, any white on the body or points, and any heavy marks (stripes or bars) on the body or legs are constituted as faults. The latter does not apply of course to the Tabby (Lynx in CFA) point, which must have distinct stripes on its mask and legs.

The following colors are brief descriptions based on the standards of the Governing Council of the Cat Fancy (GCCF) in Great Britain and of the Cat Fanciers Association (CFA) of the USA. You are recommended to obtain the full show standards of

The chocolate point Siamese has an ivory-colored body. Owner, Norma Volpe.

the registration body that you join if you wish to read the full descriptions.

•*Seal Point*— Body: pale fawn to cream. Points: dense seal brown. Nose leathers & paw pads: seal brown.

•*Chocolate Point*— Body: ivory all over. Points: milk chocolate. Nose leather & paw pads: chocolate or pinkish, chocolate (GCCF), cinnamon pink (CFA).

•*Blue Point*— Body: glacial white (GCCF), bluish white (CFA) Points: light blue (GCCF), deep blue (CFA). Nose leather & paw pads: blue (GCCF), slate blue (CFA).

•*Lilac (Frost) Point*— Body: off white (magnolia) (GCCF), glacial

Lilac point Siamese are a dilution of blue points and are quite rare and beautiful. Owner, Susan Ross.

Blue point Siamese cats have a glacial white or magnolia-colored body. Their points range from light blue to deep blue.

white (CFA). Points: pinkish grey (GCCF), frosty gray with a pinkish toe (CFA). Nose leather & paw pads: pinkish/faded grey (GCCF), lavender pink (CFA)

The following colors are accepted as Siamese in the UK and most bodies in the USA, but are called Colorpoint Shorthairs in the CFA.

•*Red Point*— Body: white shading to apricot. Points: bright reddish gold (GCCF), bright apricot to deep red (CFA). Nose leather & paw pads: pink.

•*Cream Point*— Body: white shading to pale cream. Points: cream barring & striping on mask, legs, and tail permissible (GCCF) but undesirable (CFA). Nose leather & paw pads: pink.

The lynx, or tabby point, Siamese is easily identified by the clearly defined stripes on the head, especially around the eyes and nose.

contrast with the paler background color. The tail should feature many variably sized rings, terminating in a solid colored tip. A tail with insufficient rings is regarded as a fault in this variety. Nose leather & paw pads: should match the color of the points, be a mixture of the color and pink, or be pink. The lighter the color of the points the more pinkish will be the nose leather and pads. The eye lids should tone nicely with the color of the points. Colors: may be seen in any of the recognized Siamese colors (i.e., Seal Tabby Point, Blue Tabby Point, Red Tabby Point, and so on).

•*Tabby (Lynx) Point*— Body: should be as free as possible from shading and markings, especially on the back of the head and the neck. However, some shading is to be expected, especially in the seal color. Such shading will usually be in the form of ghost striping. The applicable color should conform to that already described for the Siamese. Points: will be clearly defined stripes on the mask, especially around the eyes and nose. The whisker pads are spotted, and there are distinct marks on the cheeks. There should be no stripes on the ears — only a "thumbmark." The legs should feature clearly defined broken stripes that show good

•*Tortie Point*— Body: is as for the Tabby (Lynx) Point, but it may become mottled in older cats. Points: the ears are mottled or patched, as are the nose leather and paw pads. The tail is as for the Tabby Point, but if it is mottled this is permissible. Colors: a patchwork of red and cream as follows: Tortie Tabby Point - points patched with red and/or cream over the tabby pattern. The patching of the colors is immaterial because the breeder cannot control the placing of this by selective breeding. This means the red and cream are random in

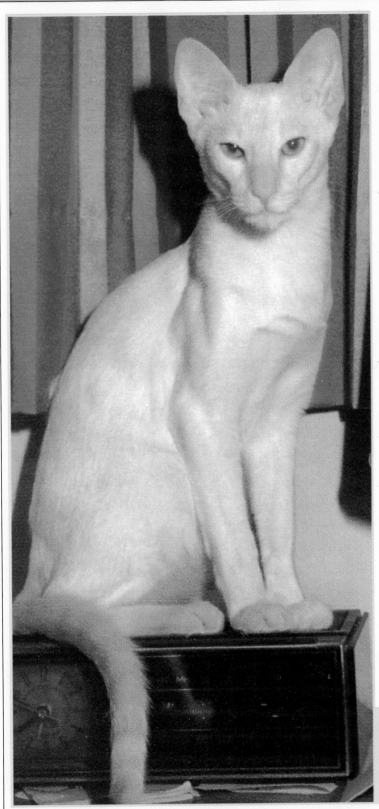

nature. Seal Tortie Point - points are variably patched with red on the seal background. Large areas of red may exhibit some striping. Presence or absence of a blaze is unimportant in the UK, but is desirable in the USA (CFA). Chocolate Tortie Point - points patched with red and/or cream on milk chocolate ground. Blue Tortie Point (called Blue-Cream Point by CFA) - points patched with cream on blue ground. Lilac Tortie Point (Lilac-Cream Point CFA) - points patched with cream.

As the tortoiseshell color is derived via sex linked genes, all torties are females.

J-Bars Maid Marion of Saroko, a red point Siamese. Owner, Dr. Robert C. Koestler.

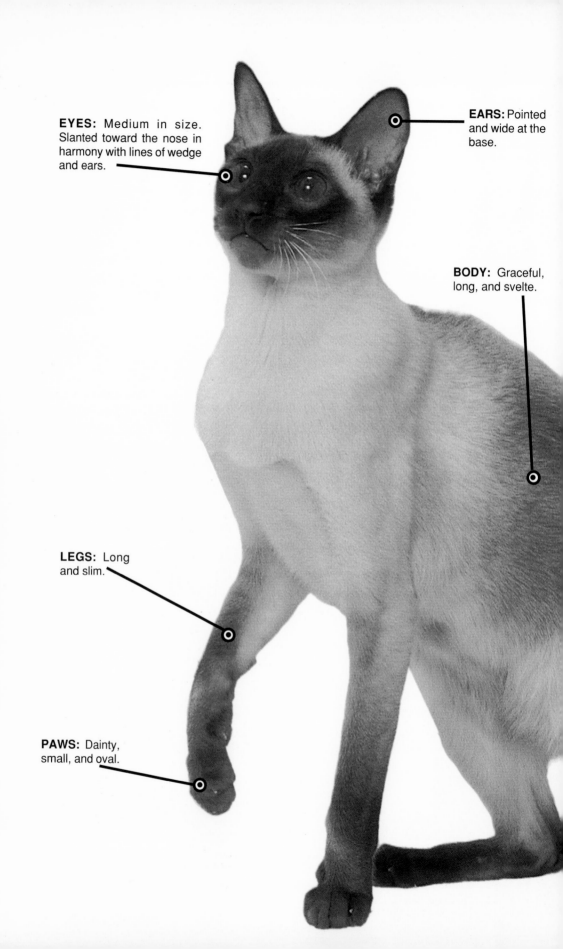

EYES: Medium in size. Slanted toward the nose in harmony with lines of wedge and ears.

EARS: Pointed and wide at the base.

BODY: Graceful, long, and svelte.

LEGS: Long and slim.

PAWS: Dainty, small, and oval.

TAIL: Long, thin, and tapering to a fine point.

The following standard for the Siamese cat is that of the Cat Fanciers' Association and is reproduced through courtesy of that organization.

SIAMESE STANDARD

General

The ideal Siamese is a medium sized, svelte, refined cat with long tapering lines, very lithe but muscular. Males may be proportionately larger.

Head

A long tapering wedge, it is medium in size and in good proportion to the body. The total wedge starts at the nose and flares out in straight lines to the tips of the ears forming a triangle, with no breaks at the whiskers. No less than the width of an eye between the eyes. When the whiskers are smoothed back, the underlying bone structure is apparent. Allowance must be made for jowls in the stud cat.

Skull

The skull is flat, and in profile, a long straight line is seen from the top of the head to the tip of the nose. No bulge over eyes. No dip in nose.

Ears

Strikingly large, the ears are pointed and wide at the base; continuing the lines of the wedge.

Eyes

Almond shaped and medium in size, the eyes are neither protruding nor recessed. Slanted towards the nose in harmony with lines of wedge and ears. Uncrossed.

Nose

Long and straight. A continuation of the forehead with no break.

Muzzle

Fine and wedge shaped.

Chin and Jaw

Medium sized, the tip of the chin lines up with the tip of the nose in the same vertical plane. Neither receding nor excessively massive.

Body

Medium sized. Graceful, long, and svelte. A distinctive combination of fine bones and firm muscles. Shoulders and hips continue same sleek lines of tubular body. Hips never wider than shoulders. Abdomen tight.

Neck

Long and slender.

Legs

Long and slim. Hind legs higher than front. In good proportion to body.

Paws

Dainty, small, and oval. Five toes in front and four behind.

Tail

Long, thin, tapering to a fine point.

Coat

Short, fine textured, glossy. Lying close to body.

Condition

Excellent physical condition. Eyes clear. Muscular, strong, and lithe. Neither flabby nor bony. Not fat.

Color

Body: even, with subtle shading when allowed. Allowance should be made for darker color in older cats as Siamese generally darken with age, but there must be definite contrast between body color and points. *Points:* mask, ears, legs, feet, tail dense and clearly defined. All of the same shade. Mask covers entire face including whisker pads and is connected to ears by tracings. Mask should not extend over the top of the head. No ticking or white hairs in points.

Penalize

Improper (i.e., off-color or spotted) nose leather or paw pads. Soft or mushy body.

Disqualify

Any evidence of illness or poor health. Weak hind legs. Mouth breathing due to nasal obstruction or poor occlusion. Emaciation. Visible kink. Eyes other than blue. White toes and/ or feet. Incorrect number of toes. Malocclusion resulting in either undershot or overshot chin. Long hair.

Siamese Colors

Seal Point: body even pale fawn to cream, warm in tone, shading gradually into lighter color on the stomach and chest. Points deep seal brown. Nose leather and paw pads—same color as points. Eye color—deep vivid blue.

Chocolate Point: body ivory with no shading. Points milk-chocolate color, warm in tone. Nose leather and paw pads—cinnamon-pink. Eye color—deep vivid blue.

Blue Point: body bluish white, cold in tone, shading gradually to white on stomach and chest. Points deep blue. Nose leather and paw pads—slate colored. Eye color—deep vivid blue.

Lilac Point: body glacial white with no shading. Points frosty grey with pinkish tone. Nose leather and paw pads—lavender-pink. Eye color—deep vivid blue.

Point Score

Head	(20)
Long, flat profile	6
Wedge, fine muzzle, size	5
Ears	4
Chin	3
Width between eyes	2
Eyes	(10)
Shape, size, slant, and placement	10
Body	(30)
Structure and size, including neck	12
Muscle tone	10
Legs and feet	5
Tail	3
Coat	(10)
Color	(30)
Body color	10
Point color (matching points of dense color, proper foot pads and nose leather)	10
Eye color	10

There are no allowable outcross breeds for the Siamese.

EXHIBITING SIAMESE

From the first time cats were seriously exhibited in London in 1871, the cat show has been the very heart of the fancy. It is the place where breeders can have the merits of their stock assessed in a competitive framework, where all cat lovers can meet and discuss ideas, trends and needs, and where new products for cats can be promoted. It is the only event in which you have the opportunity of seeing just about every color and pattern variety that exists in the Siamese breed.

Even if you have no plans to become a breeder or exhibitor, you should visit at least one or two cat shows to see what a quality Siamese looks like.

The Siamese is among the most popular of exhibition cats and has won many Best in Show awards. Both the US and Great Britain boast thousands of Siamese registrations—the breed rivals the Persian for the country's "top cat."

TYPES OF SHOW

Shows range from the small informal affairs that attract a largely local entry to the major all-breed championships and specialty exhibitions that can be spread over two or more days (but only one in Britain). A specialty is a show restricted either by breed or by hair length (short or long). In the US, it is quite common for two or more shows to run concurrently at the same site.

SHOW CLASSES

The number of classes staged at a given show will obviously reflect its size, but the classes fall into various major divisions. These are championships for whole cats, premierships for altered cats, open classes for both of the previous cats, kittens, and household pets. In all but the pet class, there are separate classes for males and females. There are then classes for all of the color and pattern varieties. At a small show, the color/patterns may be grouped into fewer classes than at a major show.

All classes are judged against the standard for the breed, other than pet classes, in which the exhibits are judged on the basis of condition and general appeal, or uniqueness of pattern. An unregistered Siamese can be entered into a pet class, and it will be judged on the same basis as would a mixed breed. A kitten in the US is a cat of four months of age but under eight months on the day of a show. In Britain, a kitten is a cat of three or more months and under nine months on the show day.

AWARDS AND PRIZES

The major awards in cats are those of Champion and Grand Champion, Premier and Grand

Siamese cats are judged against the standard of perfection, not against each other. A winning cat is the one that comes closest to conforming to "the perfect Siamese."

Premier. In Britain, a cat must win three challenge certificates under different judges to become a champion, while in the US it must win six winner's ribbons. In both instances, these awards are won via the open class. Once a cat is a champion, it then competes in the champions' class and becomes a grand based on points earned in defeating other champions. The prizes can range from certificates, ribbons and cups, to trophies and cash.

Wins in kitten classes do not count toward champion status. Champion status in one association does not carry over to another, in which a cat would have to win its title again based on the rules of that association. The rules of competition are complex, and any would-be exhibitor should obtain a copy of them from their particular registry.

The general format of cat shows, while differing somewhat from one country to another, is much the same in broad terms. A Siamese will enter its color or pattern class. If it wins, it will progress to compete against the other group winners in its breed, and ultimately compete for best of breed. If classes have been scheduled for all of the recognized colors and patterns in all of the recognized breeds, then a Best in Show will be the ultimate award. The Best in Show (BIS) is the highest honor that a cat can receive and the dream of every cat exhibitor.

JUDGING

As stated earlier, cats are judged against their written standard rather than against each other. A winning cat is one that records the highest total of points, or, put another way, the least number of demerit marks. In the US, cats are taken to the judge's table for assessment, but in Britain the judge moves around the pens with a trolley. In the US, judging is done in front of the public, but in the UK judging is normally done before the public is allowed into the hall. The exhibit owners are requested to leave the hall during judging.

CAT PENS

When you arrive at the cat show, a pen will be allocated to your cat. This is an all-wire cage. In Britain, the rules governing what can be placed into the cage are very rigid. This is because there can be no means of identifying the owner of the cat when the judge arrives at that pen. Thus, the blanket, the litter box and the water vessel must all be white. In the US the pens are highly decorated with silks, gorgeous cushions, and so on because the cat is taken to another pen for judging.

THE EXHIBITION SIAMESE

Obviously, a Siamese show cat must be a very sound example of its breed. Its coat must be in truly beautiful condition because the level of competition is extremely high at the major events. At more local affairs, the quality will not be as high, which gives more exhibitors a chance to pick up victories in the absence of the top cats of the country. The male cat